Canto familiar

Also by Gary Soto

Mercy on These Teenage Chimps

A Fire in My Hands

Accidental Love

Help Wanted: Stories

The Afterlife

Petty Crimes

Buried Onions

Novio Boy: A Play

Jesse

Local News

Pacific Crossing

Neighborhood Odes

Taking Sides

Baseball in April and Other Stories

Gary Soto

Canto familiar

Illustrated by Annika Nelson

Harcourt, Inc.

Orlando   Austin   New York   San Diego   Toronto   London

The Library of Congress has cataloged the hardcover edition as follows:
Soto, Gary.
Canto familiar/Gary Soto; illustrated by Annika Nelson.
p.   cm.
Summary: Twenty-five poems about the pleasures and woes
that Mexican American children experience growing up.
1. Mexican American children—Juvenile poetry.
2. Children's poetry, American. [1. Mexican Americans—Poetry.
2. American poetry.] I. Nelson, Annika, illus. II. Title.
PS3569.072C36 1995
811'.54—dc20   94-24218
ISBN 978-0-15-200067-7
ISBN 978-0-15-205885-2 pb

The text was set in Perpetua.
Designed by Lisa Peters

A B C D E F G H

Printed in the United States of America

Contents

Papi's Menudo 1

Spanish 4

Sarape 7

Left Shoe on the Right Foot 10

Eyeglasses 14

Music for Fun and Profit 18

My Cactus 22

Pleitos 23

¿Qué hora es? 27

Stars 29

Tortillas Like Africa 31

Handcuffs 34

Christmas Angel 38

Ironing 42

Winter Cold 46

Nopales 48

Ballet folklórico 53

My Teacher in the Market 58

Eraser and School Clock 62

Doing Dishes 65

Furnace 69

Sandía 72

Es verdad 75

Eating While Reading 76

The Good Luck Kitten 77

Canto
familiar

Papi's Menudo

It's served
On Sunday,
Just as Papi
Wakes with
Red in his eyes
And whiskers
The color
Of iron filings
Standing up
On a magnet.
It comes in
A yellow pot,
A curl of steam
Unraveling
When you lift
The lid and look in:
Tripas wagging
Like tongues
On the bottom
When you take
A spoon and stir,
Stir, dip,
And stir. Sunday,
Steam fogs the kitchen

Window. The Mexican
Station is
Starting up
Its eight violins.
Papi could cry
From the whine
Of these violins,
But it's too early.
Papi leans over
The table and
Runs a hand
Over his sleepy face.
When Mami sets
A bowl in front
Of him, he sits up
Like a good boy.
He squeezes
The lemon until
It collapses
Like a clown's frown.
He sprinkles
His *menudo* with onion
And rubs oregano
Between his lucky palms.
He roars, *¡Qué rico!*
He lifts his spoon
And blows. He

Slurps and hisses,
A slither of *tripas*
Riding down the
Chute of his throat.
He tears a piece
Of tortilla
And dips into his *menudo,*
Medicine on Sunday
When he worked
With both hands
On Saturday. Now
It's morning.
I sit next
To my bear of
A father. When
He slurps,
I slurp, stirring
Awake the whiskers
Of my cat, Hambre.
His greedy cat eyes
Spring open,
And he leaps
To his feet,
Nudging first
My legs, then Papi's,
Meowing for the love of tortilla
Dipped three times in *menudo.*

Spanish

Spanish is a matter
Of rolling *rrrrrs,*
Clicking the tongue,
And placing
Your hands
On your hips
When your little brother
Pours cereal
Into your fishbowl.
Spanish is a matter
Of yelling, *"¡Abuela,*
Teléfono! Una vendedora
De TV Guide."
It's a matter
Of Saturdays, too.
You enter the confessional
And whisper
To the priest
First the sins
You did in English,
Like screaming at the boy
On the blue bike,
And then muttering
Your sins in Spanish,

Like when you
Put on lipstick
And had bad thoughts about Mercedes Lopez,
That big show-off in new jeans.
Spanish is a matter
Of *"¡Ay Dios!"*
When the beans burn
Or *"¡Chihuahua!"*
When the weakest kid
Hits a home run.
Spanish is a matter
Of your *abuelo*
And his *compa*
Chuckling about their younger days
While playing checkers
Under the grape arbor,
Their faces lined
And dark as the earth
At their feet.
Spanish words march across
A bag of
Chicharrones,
Those salty clubs
That could easily hammer a nail
Through the wall,
They're so hard.
You've always known

Spanish, even
Behind the bars
Of your crib
When you babbled,
Mami, papi, flor, cocos—
Nonsense in the middle of the night.
At school, your friends
Have to learn Spanish,
Tripping over *gato,*
Y perro, easy words
You learned
When you looked out
The back window.
You're good at Spanish,
And even better at math.
When you walk home,
Dragging a stick
Through the rain puddles,
Spanish is seeing double.
The world is twice the size
And, with each year,
With one more candle
On a crooked cake,
Getting bigger.

Sarape

It's itchy
Against my skin,
This sarape
In the backseat
Of our Chevy,
Faded Aztec rainbow
That was a hand-me-down
From a friend
Of a friend
That Papi no longer remembers.
I get up on my knees
And look out the
Car window. The sky
Is the color of
Pencil markings
On paper,
Gray, so gray.
The wind has stripped
The apple blossoms
From the trees
And thrown them
Back into the damp earth.
We're off to a picnic,
And the piles

Of clouds may
Roll over our play.

Papi parks the car,
The windshield
With its trail of first raindrops.
We get out, me and my cousin,
Pulling on the sarape.
Each of us takes a side.
We want to throw
Bebé skyward,
And let his laughter
Scare away the clouds,
Now rolling west. We waited
Two weeks for this picnic.
We need this sarape
And *bebé* tossed into the air,
His tiny fists
Like the buds of blossoms
Breaking open.
I would like to throw
This sarape
Into the air,
And drench the sky
With ancient color.

Left Shoe on the Right Foot

Once, for fun,
I wore my shoes
On the wrong feet,
And walked
Around the back-
Yard, bowlegged,
A horse of air
Between my legs.
I laughed,
And my gum dropped
From my mouth.
My brother laughed,
And gum dropped
From his mouth, too,
Little brother
With squares of
Dark where his
Baby teeth once shone.
When he put his shoes
On the wrong feet,
We played soccer
With a flat ball—
A ball that had seen
A rosebush

And its throat of
Bitter thorns. Still,
We played, my brother
And me, now spitting
Shells of sunflower seeds.
It was fun running
Around the yard,
Our shoes pointing
In a strange, strange way.
I scored a goal,
And he scored
A goal, one after
Another, until
A lather of sweat
Gathered on our
Necks and we rested.
The fog of our
Breathing flew
Up in the winter sky.
We slipped our
Coats on backward,
The zippers running
Along our spines,
And instead of
Running forward
We ran backward,
Kicking the ball

With our heels.
Neither of us
Scored a goal.
We laughed and
Spit sunflower shells,
Until I ran into
The clothesline
And hit the back
Of my head,
A hot lump rising
Like the peeking head
Of a turtle.
Brother asked,
Does it hurt?
And I said
Just a little bit.
I got up, touching
My head, and walked
Backward into the house
And into the bed,
My shoes on
The wrong feet,
Everything dizzy
Like a wet sock spinning
In the dryer. The next day,
With my shoes
On the right feet

And my coat
Facing forward,
I got a lump on
The front of
My head, a balance
Of hurts, one
In front, one
In back, and both knocks
Straightening my bad ways.

Eyeglasses

They were
In my lunch,
And now they're lost,
My eyeglasses
That were a week old.
I remember hiding
Them when I got
To school. I put them
In my lunch
Between an orange
And a sandwich,
Tuna, I think.
But I lost them.
Now I'm almost blind,
The numbers
On the blackboard
A squiggle of nonsense.
I can barely see
My best friend
Across the room,
Or is it that girl
Who cut her hair
By herself,
Bangs like a yank of straw?

The bell rings.
I go outside,
Looking down.
When I look up,
The trees are
A blur of leaves,
And rain is starting
To fall, gently,
Like a tap
On the shoulder.
Where in the world are they?
I walk around
The school yard.
When I see
A bag blow across
The grass, I run
After it. But
Every bag is empty.
I'm in trouble.
What will Mom say
At the dinner table?
What will Dad say
After he pushes
His own glasses
Back on his nose?
I walk around
The school yard,

Rain blowing
The fall leaves
From the trees.
I'm in trouble.
I wish I were
A sparrow, or an eagle,
Some sharp-eyed bird
That can flap its wings
And soar away.
From tree level
It could spot
A pair of glasses
Peeking blindly
Through a bag.

Music for Fun and Profit

I love music.
I made a drum
Out of an oatmeal box
And a harmonica
Out of my comb and wax paper.
I made a flute
From a straw,
A triangle from
A coat hanger,
And with rubber bands
Between my thumb
And a finger,
I twanged out
"Michael Row the Boat Ashore"
To my cousin Enrique,
Cholito behind
The bars of his crib.
With pencils,
I clapped out
"Las Mañanitas"
On pie tins
And shook maracas
Of soup cans
And a handful of BBs.

With my fingers
In my mouth
I whistled
"Ol' Man River"
As I walked
To school,
Kicking through leaves
And the applause
Of cat-and-dog rain.
I made a guitar
From a shoebox
And fish line,
And strummed
"Louie Louie"
To my low-riding cat
Chato as he slunk
About the yard,
A blue bandanna
Around his neck.
I sang along
To the radio,
Slapping a beat
From my thighs.
I whistled
Through my nose
And popped a bass
From my puffed-up cheek.

———

Yes, I love music,
But I upset my *papi*
When I did a drumroll
With my spoon
And fork
As the food arrived
At the kitchen table.
I *really* upset my parents
When I spent two dollars
And a bubble gum wrapper
For a kazoo,
A flute
That sounds like a duck.

Music is fun,
And it's also for profit.
Every time I bring out
My shoe-box guitar,
My oatmeal drum,
My harmonica comb
With its skirt
Of wax paper,
Or especially my kazoo,
Papi shakes his head
And growls. He rattles
His newspaper and yells

¡Por favor, cállate!
He punches his fist
Into his pocket
And brings out
A quarter or a dime,
And I run away
With the music
Of money jingling
In my pocket.
Fun and profit!
Already I'm the lead singer
Of my own band.

My Cactus

My cactus stands in a soup can,
Packed in dirt, a gift from my *abuelo.*

My cactus is a paddle of spines.
My cactus is a paperweight for my homework.

My cactus is as old as rock,
Green as a frog, short as a big girl's thumb.

I shoo away ants and spiders.
I place it in the window, where it looks up to the trees.
I beg and coo, "Come on, let's grow, *escuincle!*"

Once, I took my cactus
In the car. Papi drove to Yosemite,
Dark shadows running over its many rivers.
My cactus got carsick but couldn't tell me.
It almost collapsed like an evil witch.

Now I know better.
I speak for my cactus.
When I rub my arm against it, I scream, "Ow!"
That's the language of cactus,
"*¡Ay, Dios!* Ouch!"

Pleitos

Pleitos, my *gatito*
With all nine lives,
Wrestles socks, bullies
A spool of yellow thread,
Boxes a potted
Plant in the corner,
And now sleeps in sunlight.
His whiskers twitch,
And his ears, left
First, then right,
Also twitch. His
Breathing comes and goes,
Comes and goes,
As the motor inside
His belly idles.
When he wakes,
He shakes a dream
From a paw,
Leaps to his feet,
And thumps about the house.
He jumps when he hears
A chair scrape in the kitchen.
He jumps when the oven
Door squeaks open.

He jumps when a spoon
Beats a pan of cold mush.
Pleitos, my *gatito*
With all nine lives,
Wrestler of dirty socks
And yarn, snarls
At the fly on the window,
The coat hanger on the door,
And the slipper knocked
On its side in the hallway.
He snarls and hisses,
And strikes the air.
He is fierce king of the house
Until he climbs
The curtain, claws
Deep into the cloth.
Then he cries,
Scared of falling.
He meows and meows,
This kitty with the hiss
Of a squeeze toy. Now
He hangs, by threads
And a prayer, and one of
His lives, it seems,
Drops as he drops—*thunk*—to the floor.
He shakes his head
And looks about,

Dizzy as a spinning dryer.
When he spies the spool
Of thread, he hisses
And creeps toward the spool,
Yellow to the core,
And an easy catch
When he leaps, face first,
Eight lives left
And every tooth gleaming.

¿Qué hora es?

I'm going to church in my best clothes.
My watch sparkles on my wrist,
Shiny as a spoon
But broken and stopped on 5:45.

I walk, staring at my watch—it's so beautiful.
A man stops me and asks, *"¿Qué hora es?"*

I look down at my watch.
I wince because the sun is bright as a knife,
And I answer, *"Señor, son las seis menos cuarto."*

A woman stops me and asks, *"¿Qué hora es, hija?"*
I tell her, *"Señora, falta un cuarto para las seis."*

A sweaty boy with a basketball hollers
From across the street, "Hey, girl, what time is it?"
I yell, "It's quarter to six, boy!"

El señor and la señora,
The boy with moons of mud on his knees
—they must think I'm *loca!*

But it's the truth.
My watch, shiny as a spoon, *no sirve!*
It's broken and forever stopped on 5:45.

How can I lie when I'm off to church?

S t a r s

I got a gold star for reading a book
And a blue star for math.

I got a bronze star
For remembering six of the nine planets circling above.
I peeled it off my test
And wore it home on my knee.

I got stars for my handwriting,
And a star for spelling *hippopotamus*
With my eyes closed.

I like the light these foil stars give off,
Shiny as spoons.

My homework piles up, a galaxy of stars.
I'm good at school.
I bet I could even get a star for eating my lunch—
My sandwich sticking to the roof of my mouth.

Where do stars come from?
From a blast of light in outer space?
From billions of years of heavenly flight?
No, they come from the store,
Or so I learned.

Now I have my own box of stars.
Every time I feel bad, I can lick a star
And just press it to my bedroom wall.

When I forget to pick up my socks, I get a star.
When I spill my milk, I get a star.
When someone calls me a name,
I get a star where it hurts, right on my heart.

Stars for kickball and the times I feel good.
Stars for when I jump from the chicken coop.
Stars when I clap my hands and my cat meows
    from the roof.
Stars when my kite swings its moon face in the air.

I'm my own teacher, my own student.
I can speak in Spanish.
I can say, *Las estrellas danzan en mis paredes.*

This happens when I turn off the lights.
At night, I blink my flashlight,
And a hocus-pocus of stars comes alive on the walls,
All shiny, all floating, all orbiting my sleep.

Tortillas Like Africa

When Isaac and me squeezed dough over a
      mixing bowl,
When we dusted the cutting board with flour,
When we spanked and palmed our balls of dough,
When we said, "Here goes,"
And began rolling out tortillas,
We giggled because ours came out not round,
      like Mama's,
But in the shapes of faraway lands.

Here was Africa, here was Colombia and Greenland.
Here was Italy, the boot country,
And here was México, our homeland to the south.

Here was Chile, thin as a tie.
Here was France, square as a hat.
Here was Australia, with patches of jumping kangaroos.

We rolled out our tortillas on the board
And laughed when we threw them on the *comal,*
These tortillas that were not round as a pocked moon,
But the twist and stretch of the earth taking shape.

———

So we made our first batch of tortillas, laughing.
So we wrapped them in a dish towel.
So we buttered and rolled two each
And sat on the front porch—
Butter ran down our arms and our faces shone.

I asked Isaac, "How's yours?"
He cleared his throat and opened his tortilla.
He said, "*¡Bueno!* Greenland tastes like México."

Handcuffs

How could I know
That when I slipped
Into handcuffs,
The plastic kind,
Mom would be gone, Father
Already on his forklift
At work? I slipped
Them on, and
Looked up
At the clock
In the kitchen,
Its big hand washing
Its face over
And over.
It was 8:23,
Seven minutes
Before I had to
Cross the street
And join my friends,
Those *changos*
On the monkey bars.
I pulled at
The handcuffs,
Yanked until my skin

Became pink
As a sock
In the wrong wash.
I banged them
On the washer,
Then the edge of
The sink, and finally
On the back porch
Until our neighbor,
Señora Cisneros,
Came out of the house,
A basket of
Steaming laundry
On one hip
And a baby
On the other.
I returned inside.
I looked for
The key,
But found only
A quarter
With a beard of grime.
The clock was still
Washing its face
Over and over
But faster.
I told myself

Not to cry,
But I cried anyway
Because I had
To go to school
With my wrists trapped.
How could I color
With these things on?
How could I raise
My hand when
I knew what was 3×4?
How could I pull
My hair out
Of my face
And turn the knob
Of the drinking fountain
At the same time?
I was in trouble,
More trouble
Than the time I burned
A note from the teacher
On our front lawn.
I think of praying,
But who is the saint of
Third Graders in Handcuffs?
I wipe my eyes.
I pick up my backpack
And take my lunch bag

Into my teeth.
My lunch wags
Under my chin
As I kick
The door closed.
I stomp down
The splintery front steps,
And, looking both ways,
Cross the street.
I start off
The day with wrists
Locked together
And palms
Not clapping
But spanking each other,
A prisoner
Of bad luck
And a lost key.

Christmas Angel

Angel cries
In his crib,
And I bring
Him a star-shaped cookie.
He takes the cookie,
And I shake
His free hand,
Little brother
Who's six months
New, his hair
Soft as warm water
Over a wrist.
I give him the cookie
And say, "This is
Your first Christmas."
A point breaks
From the cookie,
And I shove crumbs
Into his toothless mouth.
I tell Angel
About Mary
And Joseph,
And he squeals,
"Tan-tan."

I tell him
About Bethlehem
And the three wise men,
The sheep and lambs,
The shepherds
Kneeling in straw.
He squeals, "Ha-ha."
I tell him about
The star that
Shined over
The manger,
And the gifts
Placed at Baby Jesus' feet.
Angel pops his thumb
Out of his mouth
And sneezes at my story,
Little wise guy
In diapers.
I break another point
And then another
From the star cookie,
And now there are
Only two points,
Just like us,
Hermana and *hermano*.
"Angel," I whisper,
"For Christmas

I got you a duck
For the bathtub.
Can you say *duck?*"
Angel says through
His chewing, "Mo, mo."
I shake my head
And laugh. He says,
"Ba-ba, mi-mi,
Ma-ma," before
It's back to "Tan-tan."
I touch his nose
With the cookie
And pull it away.
Angel is six months
New and doesn't
Know much, only
The sweetness
Of a star-shaped cookie.
It dances over his crib,
Just beyond
His first words
And his pudgy fingers.

Ironing

Once a week,
I haul the
Laundry basket
From my closet,
Unfold the squeaky
Ironing board,
And spank the flat
Of the iron
With my palm.
It's always hot,
And heavy as stone.
This is my chore—
To smooth over
The wrinkles
Of washed clothes.
I breathe in
And I breathe out,
While the hot iron
Snorts like a bull.
I snap my shirt,
And smother the
Sleeves with steam,
Washing away the wrinkles.
Next, I iron the front,

Then the back,
Which no one sees,
And finally the collar,
Halo of stubborn dirt.
I do my two T-shirts.
I do my three jeans,
Worn at the knees
From my head-over-heels
Cartwheels
On muddy grass.
I don't like ironing.
No one likes ironing.
Why else would
The ironing board
Squeak in pain
And the iron snort
And throw out
A bad temper
Of stinky steam?
Still, it's my chore,
And my weekly gift
To my mom. Once,
For an art contest,
I wanted to dress up my drawing
Of snowy field
And two cows
Throat-deep in white.

I wanted to get rid
Of wrinkles and folds
And win! But
The heat yellowed
My snowy field,
Branded the cows
With a little bit
Of brown,
And made me cry.
Two dime-size tears
Leaped on the iron,
Which spit them back
In a puff of angry steam.

Winter Cold

I cough when I bend and wiggle my foot into a sock.
I sneeze when I squeeze a snake of toothpaste.
I cough and sneeze, and pull on brother's gloves.

Off to school, I blow my nose on the run.
At a corner, I shiver like a tree,
Even in my warmest jacket,
And my breath hangs white in the air.

I've never been so sick.
True, once I sprained my ankle when I jumped
    from a roof.
True, I hurt my toe when I kicked a chair.
True, my heart broke when the neighbor's dog
    ran away,
His waterbowl like a Frisbee in his mouth.

I wish I were a doctor.
I sneeze and cough, and my nose runs.
Now I'm sick as a wet puppy.

I should have stayed in bed,
With the covers up to my throat.
But I memorized the important rivers of the world,

And today it's girls against boys in geography.
I'm a girl in jeans. I know more than the boys,
All in a row. My friends need me—
Raquel, Margie, and Belinda.

I jump over rain puddles.
My head is filled with every river that flows—
The Nile, the Amazon, the Danube, the Seine, the
    Orinoco,
The Mississippi that the boys can't even spell.
I know small rivers that slow
To a trickle of gray water and two fish.

I cough and sneeze, and shiver from a cold.
I know my geography, I know my planet.
I jump over rain puddles without getting wet,
And the helpless boys are drowning in shallow rivers.

Nopales

Three *nopales* rise
In my *abuelo*'s dirt yard,
Three plants because
There are three
Of us—Hector,
María, and me.
My *abuelo* rooted them
In a jar, and they grew
And grew, like us,
I guess. But we grew
Hair and they grew
Paddles with
Stickery spines.

Now it's autumn.
Abuelito fumbles
For his pocketknife
In his khaki pants.
When he opens it,
Sunlight winks on the blade.
He winks at us,
And cuts through
A paddle of *nopal,*
Humming to himself

Or maybe to the bird
On the fence.
He hums and cuts,
And places the first paddle
On newspaper.
He cuts another, then more,
And finally when
He brings out
The step stool,
We think he's going
To climb up and
Cut the *tuna,* red bulb
That's the juice
Of every rain cloud
That passed overhead
With blimps and planes.
But no. Wiping his brow,
Furrowed like the earth
In his garden,
He sits on the stool.
He tells us
A story from his
Pueblo in Mexico,
A story of a young woman
And a handsome man
With green eyes.
They danced and danced,

And she fell in love
With him.
But suddenly, a wind
Blew out the lanterns
And when they were
Relit, she saw
Him as he was; she looked
Down and saw that
Instead of feet
He stood on chicken claws.
I scream
At this point, and
My *abuelo* laughs
And feels in his
Pocket for cough drops,
Medicine usually,
But candy after
A scary story.
Then it's back to work.
Abuelo cuts *nopales,*
And all of us—Hector,
María, and me,
Sylvia, the girl
You see jumping rope
With a lash of
Red licorice—we're helping
Gather the *nopales,*

These paddles that spank
And rake the wind.
We'll whittle
The spines and
Wash them in a pail.
Once diced, once tossed
In a black frying pan,
They poke through piles
And steaming piles of scrambled eggs.

Ballet folklórico

My friends
Know me
As the girl
In jeans
And tennis shoes
Flecked with mud.
My neighbor
Knows me
As the one
Who left skid marks
On the sidewalk
And a little spot
Of blood
From my left knee.
And my teacher
Knows me as
The second-best speller
Against the boys on
The other side
Of the classroom,
Boys with fingers
In their mouths,
Falling like bowling pins.

———

But on Saturday,
Not everyone knows
I take *ballet folklórico,*
My feet squeezed
Into shoes,
My smile caught
In the mirrors
On the wall,
And my cheeks hot
As the inside of a glove.
I love dancing,
And the ring
Of our steps
On the wooden floor.
I love my dress,
Flushed with the colors
Of México,
Twirling like an umbrella.
It's joy,
And swing of
Bodies, elbow
To elbow, dip
And swing, slap
And click of boots.
When I practice,
My hair unrolls
From its bun,

And with a bobby pin
In my mouth,
I fix it back.
I can dance
The *jarabe tapatío,*
The quick steps of
Las danzas de los listones,
Three different *Huapangos,*
Jaranas, and *sones de Veracruz,*
The *jarocho* with
My *guapo* cousin, Isaac.
If called on, I can dance
My favorite, *Los viejitos,*
"Dance of the Little Old Men."

Once, at a school carnival,
I danced "The Little Old Men."
My *abuelo* was there,
Leaning on his cane,
Eyes bright,
His face shiny
As a moon
Over a hill.
I danced behind
A mask of a *viejo,*
My steps staggering
And drunken.

I swayed
And fell, got to
One knee, and fell again,
Then tripped
Over my heels.
My dance steps
Were rickety
As a porch,
Lopsided
As a three-legged table.
I tapped my cane
And staggered,
Me, the girl
Playing a *viejo*
To laughter
And applause.
When the dance finished,
We ripped off
Our masks, bowed,
And shuffled away.
Later, my *abuelo*
Came up to me,
Tapping his cane,
One shoelace undone.
"I used to do that *danza*,"
My *abuelo* told me.
"You did?" I asked.

"Yes," he answered,
"And, *pues,* I got good at it."
He winked at me
And staggered away,
Knees buckling,
Back hunched,
And his cane
Dancing on the blacktop.

My Teacher in the Market

Who would suppose
On a Saturday
That my teacher
Would balance
Tomatoes in her hands
And sniff them
Right under my nose.
I'm María,
The girl with a Band-Aid
On each knee,
Pink scars the shape
Of check marks
On homework.
I'm hiding by the bags
Of potatoes,
Tiptoeing and curious.
I've never seen
My teacher in jeans
And a T-shirt,
And tennies with a hole
Where the little
Toe rubs. She
Bags the tomatoes
And a pinch of chiles.

She presses a thumb
Gently into ripe avocados,
Three for a dollar
Because they're black,
Black, but pretty black.
I wave to my teacher
And then duck,
Giggling. I look up.
She lifts a watermelon
Into her arms,
Melon with its army
Of seeds to spit
Across a sidewalk.
I can't imagine *her* doing *that,*
My teacher, my teacher.
She weighs nectarines
And plums, peaches
With their belly
Of itchy fur.
I wave again,
And duck. It's funny
Seeing my teacher
Drop a grape
Into her mouth,
Same mouth that says
4 times 6 is 36,
I mean 24. She lowers

The bunch of grapes
Into a plastic bag.
Then she turns
Toward the potatoes
And finds me peeking through.
When she says,
"Oh, it's María,
My little potato eyes,"
I blush and squint my eyes shut.
When I open them,
She's gone,
Her shopping cart
Now swinging
Down the aisle
Of cereals,
Leaving me,
María, little potato eyes.

Eraser and School Clock

My eraser
Is pink
And car-shaped.
It skids across
My math test,
Which is a mess of numbers,
All wrong, like
When I unscrewed
The back of my watch
And the workings
Fell out.
The teacher frowned
When she saw
The watch,
Its poor heart
Torn out. Now
I'm working
On my math,
And I think,
I think, I think
I know. I look
Up at the school clock
With its hammerlike tick.
I could tear

Open its back,
And perhaps
The springs and gears
Would jump
And time stop.
This test could stop,
And my friends
Freeze, pencils
In their hands,
Erasers, too.
All would freeze,
Including my teacher,
And I could blow
On the skid marks
Of my eraser.
I walk out
To the playground,
My eight fingers
And two thumbs
Wrapped around
A baseball bat.
The janitor
Is frozen
To his broom,
The gardener
To his lasso of
Hose and sprinkler,

And the principal
To his walkie-talkie.
I hit homer
After homer,
And they stand,
Faces frozen
And mouths open,
Their eyes maybe moving,
Maybe following
The flight
Of each sweet homer.
What a dream.
I shrug
And look around
The classroom
Of erasers and pencils,
The clock racing
My answers to the finish.

Doing Dishes

Last night
We had one pot
And three dishes.
Tonight, when it's my turn
To throw my hands
Into suds
We have a stack
Of plates
The color of chickens,
White and red.
That's what we
Had tonight—chicken *mole,*
A messy meal
That leaves stains
On your mouth
And greedy fingers.
We have plates.
We have six pots,
A jangle of
Forks and knives,
And a wooden spoon
That paddled
Through sauce
And docked on my lips

When Mom wasn't looking.
We have a rolling pin
Sticky with dough.
We have a potato peeler
And a pie pan
Where the flan
Set in its sweetness.
We have drinking glasses.
I pump the suds
And scrub,
My sponge raking
The *mole* sauce,
The *frijoles,*
The *arroz,*
The *papas.*
The dishwater
Turns orange,
And suds flatten.
I drain the water
And start again,
A curl of steam
Licking my eyebrows.
I wipe my eyebrow.
I pump my sponge.
I sweat over the suds
And wail inside
Because it's boring.

I could be doing
Nothing right now,
Or reading a magazine,
Which is almost
Like doing nothing.
But I scrub and rinse,
And am here
Leaning my belly
Against the sink
For hours, days, years. . . .
When I finally
Pull my hands
From the water,
They're puckered and old
—that's how long!

Furnace

In the morning,
I jump from bed
And huddle by the wall furnace,
A yawn of red, red coils.
I shiver in pajamas,
The bottoms printed
With galloping horses
And the top
Printed with elephants
Hurling beach balls,
A mix-and-match
Of animals I love.
It's cold this morning.
Frost clings to
The kitchen window,
And where
The sun comes up,
The frost is melting ice.
I can see my breath,
Puff of white.
I shout, "Boy, it's cold!"
And as I rub
My hands together,
I hear the animals

Of hunger inside
My growling stomach.

Once, when I was really little,
Snow layered our front lawn
With hard, hard white.
The house was cold, quiet.
I jumped from bed,
Turned on the heater,
And jumped back in bed
With my stuffed dolphin,
My bear, my cat with its tail gone,
The animals of sleep
And cuddle. I whispered
My leftover dreams,
And when I was ready,
I gathered my animals
Into my arms,
Carried them to the furnace,
And we sat in its glow.
My dolphin flipped
Its tail;
My bear growled
And rubbed his scratched eyes
With his paws,
And tailless cat *meoooooow*ed.
We raised our paws, fins,

And hands to the gust
Of furnace heat.
Even my slippers,
Twin rabbits on my feet,
Shivered to get warm.
What was happiness
More than me laughing
And my toes
Wiggling the noses
Of my rabbits?

Sandía

How did I know
That from a seed
You would grow
Into a big bomb
Of water, juice
That rains
On a trail of
Curious ants
When I lower
My face
Into your sweetness?
Papi cut you open
With a knife.
Now we're seated
On the front porch,
While the crickets
Rake noise from
Their hard thighs.
For a week
We're staying with
Mis abuelos,
Among a flutter
Of hens, the
Drying stalks
Of corn, and a breeze

That stirs alfalfa
On a hot night.
It's hot now,
And the stars
Blow across
The sky. A plane
Follows, it seems,
Its red light
Pulsating. Mom
Turns on the radio.
Dad rattles
His newspaper
On his knee.
A moth beats against
The porch light,
A ghost of orange
On our glowing faces.
I take you, my grin
Of watermelon, and walk out
Into the dark,
Spitting seeds
As I go, my chin
Sticky with juice.
And what luck!
As one seed flies,
A shooting star
Cuts across the sky.

Es verdad

Es verdad
That Papi saws two boards on Saturday morning,
That he pounds a nail and wipes his brow.

Es verdad
That Moma shakes a rug from the back steps,
That she yells, *"¡Chihuahua!"* when our cat, Slinky,
Tips over the garbage can.

Es verdad
That I pop my fist into my glove
And spit a mouthful of sunflower seeds.
I toss an invisible ball skyward and I think to myself,
I got it! I got it!
And the yapping mouth of my glove eats the ball
In one gulp.

I'm a hero.
That's why Papi saws the boards—a place for trophies.
That's why Moma shakes the rug—a king's path
    to lunch.
That's why I must first pick up the toppled garbage—
A humble beginning
And later, *quién sabe,* center field champ!

Eating While Reading

What is better
Than this book
And the churn of candy
In your mouth,
Or the balloon of bubble gum,
Or the crack of sunflower seeds,
Or the swig of soda,
Or the twist of beef jerky,
Or the slow slither
Of snow cone syrup
Running down your arms?

What is better than
This sweet dance
On the tongue,
And this book
That pulls you in?
It yells, *"Over here!"*
And you hurry along
With a red, sticky face.

The Good Luck Kitten

Three stripes
Of good luck
Saddle her back,
Four stripes crown
Her tail,
And two run
Down her throat
Like milk
Coughed up from drinking
Too quickly.

My kitten has nine stripes
—nine lives of good luck—
And at ten after twelve
She may use one:
She's on the roof
Crying, "Meooooooooow,"
While I'm eating
Lunch, a flap
Of baloney in my sandwich
And salty rafts of potato chips
On a paper towel.
I gulp my milk
And hurry outside.

I shade my brow
With a salute,
Squint and eye her eyeing me,
Beads of water
On her whiskers.

"Come down," I plead,
And stomp my foot.
But she cries
The cry of millions
Of other cats,
Cries, "Meooooooooow."
I call again
And again she cries, "Meoooooooow,"
Shaking the watery beads
From her whiskers.
I have no choice.
I prop my father's ladder
Against the roof
And climb eight wooden rungs,
My lucky number.
I snap my fingers,
Throw a kiss,
And promise
A plate of milk.
Her ears perk up,
And just like that,

She walks into my arms,
Me, the big brother
Of kittens in trouble.
I bring her down
And live up to my promise—
A puddle of milk.
And because she pumps
Her paws and meows,
I toss her a corner of my sandwich.
I love my kitten,
This spring gift with nine—
Make it eight—furry lives.